Forty Days with the Psalms: Reflections for Lent

Robert W. Rice

ISBN:
ISBN-13: 978-1542549226

DEDICATION

To all those who long to honestly pour out their hearts before the Lord

ACKNOWLEDGMENTS

After publishing an advent devotional, I had planned to put my writing on hold for awhile, returning only to my daily devotionals. However, at a council meeting late last year, my clerk, Angie, had inadvertently, or perhaps intentionally, referred to that project as a Lenten Devotional and such began the journey to this book. I'd like to thank my assistant Danielle for the many hours she spent editing and making suggestions on wording for clarity. Her comments and fixes keep this work from being the jumbled up mess that flows from my mind and heart quicker than my fingers can type. I'd also be remiss if I did not acknowledge the support of my church family and their encouragement for me to continue in my writing. My wife and children also deserve special thanks, as they always support and encourage me to continue on, even when I feel stuck or have moments of struggle.

Finally, I cannot claim that this work is my own, but the product of many hours spent in prayer listening to the Holy Spirit. Thank You Lord, for choosing to use me. May You receive all the glory!

PRAYER

Father God, You know our hearts, You know us intimately. We pray that as we read and meditate on these words, You would be with us, revealing Yourself to us, and guiding our lives by the Power of the Holy Spirit living within us. May we do all things to bring You glory. In Jesus' Name, AMEN.

FORWARD

My son, Cole, brought home a rather interesting assignment from school the other day. On the page, several items were listed and he was to group the items into one of two categories: "wants" or "needs." Overall, I think Cole did pretty well with the activity, making sure to put things like "sweet treats" and "video games" into the "wants" column, and including things like "clean water" and "shelter" into the "needs" column. I used the opportunity to talk to Cole about our most basic need, which was not listed on the paper: Jesus Christ. Without Him, all of life, even those basic needs, cease. We need Jesus more than anything. We need to have a relationship with Him in order to have life. We deepen our relationship with Jesus Christ through His Word, given to us to strengthen and feed us.

However, sometimes the line between "wants" and "needs" in our lives tends to blur, as I'm sure it did for those third graders as they worked on this paper. Sometimes it's the things we want that take precedence over those things we need. Our desire for material items challenges and strangles our deep need for a relationship with God our Father, through Jesus Christ as revealed in His Word. Life can be difficult, and no one understands that struggle in Scripture better than the Psalmist. In the Psalms, we read about struggle and trial. We see real emotion displayed but are reminded to always have our lives grounded in what matters most, turning back to God and trusting His Word.

As we enter the season of Lent, a season marked by the church to teach us what is truly necessary and the value of repentance, many people tend to find peace by removing things from their lives. By avoiding that which is merely a want, the heart can fix and focus itself on what is our true need: a relationship with God our Father through Jesus Christ, and the sacrifice that will conclude this season.

The practice of fasting from various things has come to mark this season, and you may take part in this practice in some way or another. However, fasting without focusing on what matters is meaningless, so this devotional is written that you might use these forty days (Sundays are excluded in the season of Lent) to draw closer to God, and to focus on His Word. As alluded earlier, the focus of our study will be the Psalms, which speak to our hearts and show us the many facets of the human condition. Yet it also grounds us in that which has become our daily bread. As Jesus reminds us, we don't live by bread alone, but by every Word that proceeds from the mouth of God. So join me for these forty days in reflecting on selected Psalms, so we might turn away from the trivial and focus on the Everlasting God.

DAY 1
Psalm 1:1-3
Blessed is the one
who does not walk in step with the wicked
or stand in the way that sinners take
or sit in the company of mockers,
but whose delight is in the law of the Lord,
and who meditates on his law day and night.
That person is like a tree planted by streams of water,
which yields its fruit in season
and whose leaf does not wither—
whatever they do prospers.

Each day we are faced with choices such as, "What will we do? Where will we go? What will we decide to say?" Sometimes these choices paralyze us, for we are overwhelmed and are not sure which option is best. But this need not be the case, since we can make one choice each day that will inform and influence every other part of our lives. We can choose to give the Word of God a prominent place in our lives each and every day.

Psalm 1 reminds us of the importance that the Scripture should play in our lives each day. For us to live as God intends, we need to do more than simply read the Scripture. Indeed, we need to meditate on how His Word meant to feed and change us, as the Holy Spirit uses this to mold us into Christlikeness. This can't be done in an instant. A friend and mentor of mine once said that we can't microwave the truth of Scripture, we need to slow-cook it. Only by dwelling and planting ourselves in the Word of God will we find nourishment that we need to live from day to day.

That image, of a tree planted by streams of water, is a wonderful reminder of what we should do during this season of refinement. We must resolve, much like we do at the beginning of a new year, to change our behaviors and attitudes to go beyond being with God for a few moments. We must instead be planted ourselves, and lay down roots so we might experience the depth of God's sustaining love for us. Today, let us consider what it means to delight in God, and let us choose to give our hearts, our lives, and what this day brings to Him before we make any other decision!

DAY 2
Psalm 2:1-6
Why do the nations conspire
and the peoples plot in vain?
The kings of the earth rise up
and the rulers band together
against the Lord and against his anointed, saying,
"Let us break their chains
and throw off their shackles."
The One enthroned in heaven laughs;
the Lord scoffs at them.
He rebukes them in his anger
and terrifies them in his wrath, saying,
"I have installed my king
on Zion, my holy mountain."

From His birth, Jesus has always been a controversial Messiah. Even as we prepare to remember His great sacrifice on the cross, consider that several were influenced by sin and Satan to destroy the plan of God. At the birth of Jesus, King Herod became enraged, and destroyed children to protect his earthly throne from Him who would not be an earthly king. When Jesus began to teach, His words threw even those who knew Him best into a rage and they sought to stone Him. Jesus has always been controversial, and the plan of God has always stirred rebellion in the sinful hearts of men.

This is really the heart of sin, the lie that has been planted in our hearts since the serpent spoke in the garden, that we know better than God, and would be much better off without Him. Sin tells us that what we should do is ignore God, live for ourselves, and seek to live life our way. We boast and brag at our independence and while it may work for a while, in the end even the best among us is brought to our knees and realize that we are unable to make it alone.

Rather than learning this lesson the hard way, we would do well to recognize God's Sovereignty in all things, and seek to order our lives according to His perfect plan. For if we stand against God, we will surely fall, for no matter what man may say, the plans of God are perfect and His purposes cannot be thwarted. Let us resolve today to reorder our hearts according to the truth, repenting of our selfish pride, and falling on the grace of God to transform our hearts to be fully dependent on Him.

DAY 3
Psalm 3:1-4
Lord, how many are my foes!
How many rise up against me!
Many are saying of me,
"God will not deliver him."
But you, Lord, are a shield around me,
my glory, the One who lifts my head high.
I call out to the Lord,
and he answers me from his holy mountain.

How could we contemporize the words of this Psalm? Perhaps a good first line would be, "Nobody likes me, everybody hates me...." But the Psalmist is not content to "go and eat worms" at the sight of many enemies. Instead, he turns his thoughts to God. God will surely deliver him, for God is his Shield and his glory. God pulls him from the dirt and lifts up His eyes to see the truth. His enemies are many, people are out to get him, lies abound around him, but the Psalmist will not give in. Instead, he calls out to God.

How we should be like the Psalmist, confronting God with everything that concerns us! But all too often we follow contemporary logic, and prefer to eat worms! Of course we don't actually eat worms, but we do sulk, complain, and worry about what is happening around us rather than give our cares and concerns to God. When foes surround us in the form of disease, financial trouble, and broken relationships, we are content to hang our heads and cry out to ourselves. Doubt surrounds us and rather than confront them with the truth, we embrace the lies of the enemies.

It is in these moments that we need to hear the voice of truth. We need to talk ourselves into that which is sure and certain. This is the truth: The Lord is our Shield and Protector, no eternal harm shall come to those of us who trust in Him. We can lift up our heads and hear the voice of God calling out to our hearts with love for us, His children. Today, let us open our ears to hear the voice of truth, and let us put aside the worms and feast on the daily bread that comes in the form of the Word of God!

DAY 4
Psalm 3:5
I lie down and sleep;
I wake again, because the Lord sustains me.

If you're like me, some days feel as if they will never end. There is always one more thing to be done and when my head hits the pillow I am exhausted and ready for some rest. But then the inevitable happens, my brain seems to repeat the events of the day and I begin to play out what must be done tomorrow. It's as if I can't turn things off. There is simply too much going on around me.

As rest eludes me, I'm reminded that my problem is not so much a brain issue as it is a trust issue. I need to trust the Lord to sustain me as I sleep, and trust Him as I wake again in the morning for a new day. There is no need to fear. Much like the children's prayer, I will find rest if "I pray the Lord my soul to keep."

The words of David in Psalm 3 feel as if they don't belong if you read only the opening section of the Psalm. As David is surrounded by His enemies and taunted, it seems as if David should write about the difficulties He has. But David does not struggle, for David is a man of deep trust. He knows the truth that no matter what comes, the Lord is able to sustain us and refresh us as we place ourselves in His tender care.

Like David, we will surely all have days which feel draining. We will face various struggles in this life. However, in the Lord's Presence, we can rest and be refreshed, as He sustains us day by day, no matter what comes. As we awake today, let us be strengthened for what this day brings and as we sleep tonight, let us be reassured that the Lord will restore and refresh our souls by His sustaining Presence in our lives.

DAY 5
Psalm 4:8
In peace I will lie down and sleep,
for you alone, Lord,
make me dwell in safety.

"Be safe as you sleep" sounds like it could be a catch phrase for a security company. I can almost imagine a couple laying in bed, when an intruder is scared away because of spotlights, or perhaps sirens. But security companies are not the only group trying to sell peace of mind to people today. Some people find peace of mind in their own strength, life insurance, or in firearms that protect them from whatever may come.

But there is a problem in this mindset, finding safety in ourselves or the things we trust. No matter what it is that we think will keep us safe, nothing is infallible. Security systems are breached, that which claims to be unbreakable is broken, and we ourselves are fickle and unable to stand against certain things that come against us. If we try and find safety in these things, we may sleep soundly for a while but eventually, our world may be shaken. Even if we last through our lives with no issues, not one of us can stay safe from our greatest enemy, death.

Though we can't find safety nor peace in the things of this world, these ideals are possible for us in our lives. However, peace and safety are only possible if we place our trust in the Lord. We can have peace as we give Him our hearts fully. We can know that come what may, we will be safely held in His arms. Nothing that comes can separate us from His love that is in Christ Jesus, and that is the safest place we can anchor our lives. Today, let us rest and anchor ourselves in Christ Jesus, and let us be at peace as we wake in the morning and lie down to sleep.

DAY 6
Psalm 5:3
In the morning, Lord, you hear my voice;
in the morning I lay my requests before you
and wait expectantly.

I haven't always been a morning person. Though I tend to rise early now, there were days when I would stay in bed until noon or even later. Part of the problem was a work schedule that caused me not to be home until around 1:00 a.m. The other part was sheer laziness (this is the confession my wife has been waiting on for years). I had no desire to start a new day, my life was a grind at that point, and I can say that I struggled with my prayer life.

I can't point to the exact moment, but I eventually decided I needed to change. With a lot going on during the day, I needed to make time for God in the morning. My day needed to begin with offering myself to God, and hearing from Him. I'm not perfect in my quest to rise early. Sometimes, I still get a late start, but I commit each day to begin my day in God's Word, in prayer, and then with a little physical exercise.

You don't have to get up as early as I do to have a great relationship with God, but this Psalm reminds us that the very first thing we should do is spend time in prayer. The morning is a time to speak to the Lord and be spoken to by God. It is a moment when we can give the Lord the day and all that it will bring. Christians throughout the centuries, when faced with many tasks to accomplish, have often reminded us that nothing is a substitute for prayer.

So let us commit now, to begin this and each day in a dedicated time of prayer to God. If you struggle with what to say, try personalizing each petition of the Lord's Prayer to your life. Move forward in the day, ready and waiting for God to be active in your life and see what He will do!

DAY 7
Psalm 5:5-7

**The arrogant cannot stand
in your presence.
You hate all who do wrong;
you destroy those who tell lies.
The bloodthirsty and deceitful
you, Lord, detest.
But I, by your great love,
can come into your house;
in reverence I bow down
toward your holy temple.**

In the Gospel of Luke we read the story of Jesus watching two people coming to the temple to pray (see Luke 18:10). One man boldly came in and spoke of how great he was in comparison to others. I imagine him strutting in, head held high, thinking he was hot stuff. This was self-righteous arrogance on full display, and in the eyes of Jesus, it was worthless and detestable. But a second man came in, who stood back in humble reverence and kept his head down, so as not to make a show. He begged for God's mercy and was rewarded by being justified by God.

The contrast of the two men in the story fits the contrast that is depicted in the verses above, and it reminds us of how we should approach the Presence of the Lord. We must come humbly, in awesome reverence of who He is. This Psalm reminds us that though we don't deserve to come into the Lord's Presence, we are beckoned to His Presence by His great love for us. We shouldn't take that great love for granted, and should instead come with awe and trembling to approach His throne of grace.

Unfortunately, it's easy for us to forget this great truth. Pride comes into our lives and tells us that our "goodness" gives us the right to approach the Lord. We think that we deserve something from Him. We too often, whether we realize it or not, strut into God's Presence and want Him to know how great we are. The remedy for this attitude is to remember that it is only by His love that we come to His presence. We need to humbly offer Him praise for all He has done and remember with our words of praise that it is not about us being great, but of the greatness of our God.

DAY 8
Psalm 6:1-3
Lord, do not rebuke me in your anger
or discipline me in your wrath.
Have mercy on me, Lord, for I am faint;
heal me, Lord, for my bones are in agony.
My soul is in deep anguish.
How long, Lord, how long?

I am by nature an impatient person. I can't stand things like traffic lights, speed limits, and lines. Before you condemn me, consider whether or not you recognize these or similar tendencies in your own life. I'm sure if you are honest, you will, as I have, come to grips with the fact that we all struggle with this thing called patience. The lack of this quality in the human race is part of our sinful condition. We are impatient because sin teaches us that life should revolve around our timing, and when God's timing is different we struggle.

We should not think we are alone in our struggle, for even the Psalmist struggled with God's timing. Faced with a difficult string of circumstances, he turned to God and cried out what we all think from time to time, "How long will this last?" It's that thought that goes through our minds when we see something that is in need of correction. It's the cry of our desperate hearts, sometimes through pain and tears, and it is exactly what we should give to the Lord in moments of deep distress.

We should give this pain to the Lord, because this honesty proclaims the truth. Indeed, we often lack understanding as to how the Lord is at work. It is good to come to the Lord and call upon His name for mercy, healing, deliverance, and salvation. We need all these things, and there is no other way we will find them. If we don't give our struggles and complaints to the Lord or if we can't come to His presence with all things, we will surely deal with them in other ineffective, and perhaps even sinful ways. Far better that we approach Him in prayer so that we might be led from our struggle into wisdom and a relationship with Him who gives us life and holds our lives in His hands.

DAY 9
Psalm 7:3-5
**Lord my God, if I have done this
and there is guilt on my hands—
if I have repaid my ally with evil
or without cause have robbed my foe—
then let my enemy pursue and overtake me;
let him trample my life to the ground
and make me sleep in the dust.**

Many times in my own eyes, I feel I make no mistakes. I have reasons for what I do, and if I do something that is wrong, it is surely not my fault. However, in the eyes of others, I'm not seen as perfect and infallible (at least I hope not), for I am human and a sinner who is capable of making many mistakes. Others can see the blind spots in my life and the areas of struggle far easier than I can because the sin of pride often distorts my view. It's why we need accountability in life, we need to open ourselves up to the discerning eyes of others and lay our hearts before the Lord.

In this Psalm, David opens his heart to the Lord and asks the Lord to examine him. David also, if he is in the wrong, welcomes the consequences that will come from his sin. Of course, David isn't doing this because he thinks he is in the wrong. He believes with his heart that what is happening to him is unjust. He has not treated his enemies with contempt, so he feels that he is therefore not guilty. But David isn't content with his own assessment of things. He welcomes the Lord to look upon his life, and vindicate him or punish him if necessary.

David's words are not meant to be a self-righteous prayer, but an opportunity that we often avoid, the opportunity for the Lord to look at a situation and show us what is truth. We often avoid this examination for fear that we may be wrong, but we shouldn't because even if we have sinned, and even if we deserve consequences, through Christ Jesus we can be restored to the Lord's Presence. We shall never lose His Presence or love. So today, let us call upon the Lord to look at our lives and open ourselves for Him to show us who we truly are.

DAY 10
Psalm 7:17
**I will give thanks to the Lord because of his righteousness;
I will sing the praises of the name of the Lord Most High.**

As I prepare this devotional, it's just after the Christmas holiday, and I've recently spent time writing some thank you notes for gifts that I have received. I'm not always great at this practice, but I am sure to always give thanks for what I have been given usually in person. Hopefully, you are a thankful person also. But let me suggest that our thanks should go beyond what we receive. How often have you simply said thank you to someone for who they are?

As we ponder that thought, think of all the thank you moments we find in Scripture. While many of them are based on what the Lord has done for people, this thank you is based on who the Lord is. The Lord is righteous, perfect in all of His ways. It is not about what He does, it is about who He is. The Psalmist finds value not in what He has been given, but in the fact that He serves a God who is just and right in His very being. As thanks are given for who God is, praise breaks out because of this same idea. These two actions go hand in hand.

It is a good thing to give thanks for the gifts we have been given. We must never cease to praise God for these things, but our thanksgiving must go beyond this alone. We must also thank and praise God for who He is, awesome and wonderful, powerful and mighty, just and right, and perfect in all of His ways. As we pray today, let us begin by this powerful practice, simply dwelling on who God is. As our minds and hearts are overwhelmed by His holy and awesome nature, let us break forth in praise to Him who is truly worthy not for what He has done, but for who He is.

DAY 11
Psalm 8
Lord, our Lord,
how majestic is your name in all the earth!
You have set your glory
in the heavens.
Through the praise of children and infants
you have established a stronghold against your enemies,
to silence the foe and the avenger.
When I consider your heavens,
the work of your fingers,
the moon and the stars,
which you have set in place,
what is mankind that you are mindful of them,
human beings that you care for them?
You have made them a little lower than the angels
and crowned them with glory and honor.
You made them rulers over the works of your hands;
you put everything under their feet:
all flocks and herds,
and the animals of the wild,
the birds in the sky,
and the fish in the sea,
all that swim the paths of the seas.
Lord, our Lord,
how majestic is your name in all the earth!

There is a dream in my life that is yet unfulfilled. I long some day to experience the true splendor of the stars in the heaven without the light pollution that blurs them from view. This isn't an impossible dream, there are areas (one not too far away from me) that are designated as "dark sites" where you can go and see the stars in all their glory. To this point, I've only seen pictures of the full majesty of the heavens. But even as I look into the skies and see the few stars and the moon, I can't help but be overwhelmed with the glory of God.

As I go for runs in the morning, I often take pictures of the sunrise (which is never quite the same) or of the river, or of any number of things and I am always struck by the beauty and vastness of creation. My heart is filled with praise to God, and the majesty that is displayed through His creation. It's a good feeling to have, to be struck with the awe of what we see (and don't see) and know that God is behind it all, and then remember that God cares individually for each one of us.

Unfortunately, many people look around this world, and they see not the majesty of God, but have blinded eyes. We, too, can be guilty of this if we choose to move too quickly through our day. We sometimes have eyes that are fixed and focused too much on ourselves, the problems we face, and that which is broken. It's not that these things don't exist, for the world is a broken place, but if we slow down and open our eyes to see what is around us, we will again be filled with the awesome majesty of God. We can then proclaim, "How Great is our God! How awesome is He! He made the earth and this world, yet He still cares for me!"

DAY 12
Psalm 9:7-10
The Lord reigns forever;
he has established his throne for judgment.
He rules the world in righteousness
and judges the peoples with equity.
The Lord is a refuge for the oppressed,
a stronghold in times of trouble.
Those who know your name trust in you,
for you, Lord, have never forsaken those who seek you.

I love the last verse of the song, "Joy to the World." It is a shame that we have relegated what was meant to be a hymn about the second coming, to a mere Christmas carol. The words are bold and powerful and proclaim the truth about the glorious reign of the King of Kings:

He rules the world with truth and grace
And makes the nations prove, the glories of His righteousness
And wonders of His love.

This Psalm proclaims the same great truth. No matter who may sit in places of earthly power, the Lord will always be King. His Kingdom shall never end. We can take solace in the fact that no matter what happens in this world, it shall always be temporary. Nothing can thwart the purposes or reign of the sovereign King. His purposes are perfect, ruling in truth and righteousness, and He offers us grace and protects us, His children.

Yes, He rules and reigns, and in this time as we wait for His earthly Kingdom to come, we can find refuge in His Presence. That is the wonder of His love for us, though we do not deserve it. However, through Jesus, we can enter His Presence and seek after Him, finding all that we need for this day. No matter what comes this day, or in the future, we can hold fast to the promise that is proclaimed and have joy because of it. The Lord is King! Let us seek therefore to love and serve Him today!

DAY 13
Psalm 10:1
Why, Lord, do you stand far off?
Why do you hide yourself in times of trouble?

The unanswered question, the healing that does not seem to take place, the silence, the dark night of the soul, these are all realities that seem to happen in our lives. As we read the opening words of this Psalm, we are confronted with these truths for days, weeks, or even longer. It appears that the Lord is not faithful to His promise, that somehow He has forgotten about us and left us all alone. And so, like the Psalmist, we cry out, "Why Lord?"

The truth is, there seems to be no sufficient answer to this question anywhere in Scripture. The Lord's ways are not our ways, and there are some situations and circumstances that we are not meant to understand here on this earth. So how should we respond to those moments when the question fills and haunts our minds, when reality seems to go against the truth that the Lord will never leave us nor forsake us?

The solution is not found in ignoring or minimizing what is happening. We won't find solace in clichés or catch phrases. Instead, we can only find some relief in reminding ourselves of what is true and lasting, coming to the Presence of the Lord himself. The worst thing we can do when it seems as if the Lord has abandoned us, is to abandon our prayer life. Instead, we need to remind and confront ourselves with the glory of God. We need to wait in His Presence, pour our hearts out to Him, and open our spiritual ears so we might hear Him speak to our hearts through His word.

Often when the situations mentioned above take place, we tend to close our Bibles rather than open them. Instead, let us fill our hearts with the truth and run towards the majesty of God. Let us hold fast to the fact that even though our feelings tell us otherwise, God is ever with us.

DAY 14
Psalm 11:4-7
**The Lord is in his holy temple;
the Lord is on his heavenly throne.
He observes everyone on earth;
his eyes examine them.
The Lord examines the righteous,
but the wicked, those who love violence,
he hates with a passion.
On the wicked he will rain
fiery coals and burning sulfur;
a scorching wind will be their lot.
For the Lord is righteous,
he loves justice;
the upright will see his face.**

Big brother is watching. It is a haunting thought in our society today that we can't do much of anything without someone knowing. My brother-in-law remarked that those in-home devices that are set to respond to your every command, are more like NSA listening-devices. Even those things which we think are private are probably monitored by someone. I don't say these things so you will be paranoid, but to remind you that we do nothing in secret.

And even if we do something unseen by the world, the Lord is watching and examining each of us. For some people, that can be a scary and troubling thought. The idea that the Lord is omniscient, seeing and knowing all things, is especially troubling if we find ourselves caught in wickedness. For as this Psalm reminds us, the wicked are destined for judgment, described here as fiery coals and burning sulfur.

But for those of us who have taken the righteousness of Jesus Christ upon us, the Lord looks upon us with a different purpose. He seeks to examine our lives. While an exam may not seem very pleasant, the idea behind this word is that of proving a precious metal. It is examined, but only to strip away what is not helpful and to show the purity. It is like a refinement, necessary for us to be made into the image of God.

Yes, the Lord is watching us. But He is not watching us to cause us to stumble or to rain down lightning bolts when we make a mistake. He looks upon us with love and examines us so we might be made more like Him. He displays His justice in our life and readies us by the power of the Holy Spirit day by day for heaven, where we will see His face.

DAY 15
Psalm 12:1-4
Help, Lord, for no one is faithful anymore;
those who are loyal have vanished from the human race.
Everyone lies to their neighbor;
they flatter with their lips
but harbor deception in their hearts.
May the Lord silence all flattering lips
and every boastful tongue—
those who say,
"By our tongues we will prevail;
our own lips will defend us—who is lord over us?"

One of my favorite shows on television was "House." It tells the story of the cranky and untrusting Dr. Gregory House, who has a terrible bedside manner, but was a master of solving the most complicated medical cases. In the show, one of Dr. House's favorite mantras was, "Everyone lies." While I can't agree with every one of Dr. House's assessments about humanity, this one is most definitely true.

As we read the opening to this Psalm, we may be conjuring up images of friends who have betrayed us, lies that we have believed, and we may be quite ready to prepare to stand in judgment against everyone else in this world. But the problem isn't just that other people are not faithful. The problem is that we, too, are unfaithful and part of the problem. Before we begin to point the proverbial finger at someone else as we read these words, let's first examine our own hearts.

We all, even the most righteous and honest among us, either bend the truth or outright lie from time to time. We justify our actions saying that these things are necessary for our own good or the good of others. As our lips repeat these falsehoods, we set ourselves against the Lord, Jesus Christ, who is in very nature truth. We may not realize it, but as this Psalm and other places in Scripture reveal, our tongues and the lies they tell can do great damage to our lives, and are reason for us to be judged by the Lord as sinful.

This revelation should cause us to begin this day as a confession of our own misguided hearts and motives. Like Isaiah, we should fall before the Lord this day and confess: "I am a person of unclean lips." As we make this confession, let us allow the righteousness and truthfulness of Jesus Christ to wash over us yet again and cleanse our lips. Let us seek today to tell the truth and be faithful, not in our own power, but in the power of the Spirit living within us.

DAY 16
Psalm 13
How long, Lord? Will you forget me forever?
How long will you hide your face from me?
How long must I wrestle with my thoughts
and day after day have sorrow in my heart?
How long will my enemy triumph over me?
Look on me and answer, Lord my God.
Give light to my eyes, or I will sleep in death,
and my enemy will say, "I have overcome him,"
and my foes will rejoice when I fall.
But I trust in your unfailing love;
my heart rejoices in your salvation.
I will sing the Lord's praise,
for he has been good to me.

Tucked amidst other stories in the Gospel of Luke (13:10-13), there is a story of a woman who is healed on the Sabbath after being in bondage to a weakening spirit for a period of 18 years. Consider that for just a minute. Sometimes 18 minutes seems like an eternity when we are waiting for something, yet this woman had been living in pain and weakness for 18 years. I've often wondered if she ever recited the words of this Psalm. Being a Jewish woman, she likely heard the words a time or two, but for her they took on a very vivid and real meaning.

That is the purpose of the words of Scripture. Not to remain on a page, but instead to enter our hearts and become a prayer for us. These words filled with pain and sorrow can become the real cry of our hearts living in this world of sin. We can feel forgotten and abandoned by God, and the worst thing we can do is to ignore or put that thought aside. We need to grasp it, wrestle with it, and pour it out in raw emotion before God. But like the Psalm and the woman from Luke remind us, we can't let emotion cloud our minds to the truth.

You see, though the woman had been in bondage for 18 years, Jesus found her in the synagogue, a place of prayer and worship. She hadn't given up on God. She was still trusting. It wasn't easy, it never is, but we need to remind ourselves of the truth because pain can blur it out. The Lord is good and deserves our praise. In His good and perfect purposes, at the right time, He will surely remove our pain and oppression and set all things right. But even if those things don't happen today, tomorrow, this year, or ever on this earth, let us not abandon Him who is our Salvation and who is actively working to bring us good, through the pain, and sometimes through earthly healing.

Today, let us pour our real and raw emotion out before the Lord. Let us also remind our hearts of the truth and vow to place our trust in Him, praising him, even through tears.

DAY 17
Psalm 14:1
**The fool says in his heart,
"There is no God."
They are corrupt, their deeds are vile;
there is no one who does good.**

"There is no God." How can anyone embrace such a silly and foolish thought? Why would anyone doubt God? Before we write these words off as unimportant for us, let's consider some of the reasons behind them. If there is no God, we answer to no one. If there is no God, we can do what we want. If there is no God, this life is without meaning and we should live wholly for ourselves. The statement is false, but embracing it makes life somewhat easier if you want to live for yourself. But it also removes all meaning from this life. Without God we have no purpose, no reason to live past this death. As we read in the book of Ecclesiastes, everything is meaningless, and there is no reason to live.

Yes, when considered from that perspective, it is quite foolish to make such a remark, for living like there is no God in the Presence of an All-Powerful God is a scary proposition. Surely none of us would make such a statement. Yet, sometimes we operate our lives as if there is no God, no one watching over us and out for us.

When we embrace sin, we are essentially saying that we don't care that there is a God who has standards for us to live by. When we live lives paralyzed by fear, we are essentially saying that there is not a God watching over us who is greater than all things in this world. Yes, we may never be so foolish to say such a thing, but sometimes our lives display that we are living as fools do.

How can we correct such things? We need to come into His Presence and allow Him to reveal Himself to us. As we see Him for who He is, our hearts will be filled again with awe and wonder, as well as with the realization that we have sinned against Him. We must confess our doubts and unbelief, and ask Him to help us, leading and guiding us to live in such a way that we bear witness that there is a God and that He is with us always!

DAY 18
Psalm 14:7
Oh, that salvation for Israel would come out of Zion!
When the Lord restores his people,
let Jacob rejoice and Israel be glad!

We often think of the individual aspects of salvation. We emphasize the fact that I am saved, I am delivered. Even the words of one of our favorite hymns, "Amazing Grace," that speaks of the grace of God, emphasizes the individual aspects of salvation: "Amazing grace, how sweet the sound, that saved a wretch like me."

Our relationship with God is individual in the fact that no one can make the decision to accept the grace of God for us. We can't rely on someone else's faith to save us, and just because everyone else in our family has a relationship with God, doesn't mean that we necessarily do. However, God's salvation is not meant to be lived in an individual vacuum. His grace is not given that we might remove ourselves from the community. And when we emphasize individual over community, sometimes we misunderstand the work of the Lord.

This Psalm reorients us, calling out not just for individual salvation, but for God to deliver His people as a whole. Consider that as the people of Israel prayed, it wasn't just for individual rescue, but that God would deliver the nation. It is with this realization, that God is working through and for us, that can cause great joy. This made the people glad, for their concern was not only for themselves, but for one another. Perhaps we would do well to learn from this mentality, and not just be concerned with "me," but with us.

Therefore, let us today, pray for salvation to come not just for ourselves, but for all people. Let us rejoice as God works not through us alone, but restores this earth through the body of Christ, and gives deliverance to the community and to all those who believe!

DAY 19
Psalm 15
Lord, who may dwell in your sacred tent?
Who may live on your holy mountain?
The one whose walk is blameless,
who does what is righteous,
who speaks the truth from their heart;
whose tongue utters no slander,
who does no wrong to a neighbor,
and casts no slur on others;
who despises a vile person
but honors those who fear the Lord;
who keeps an oath even when it hurts,
and does not change their mind;
who lends money to the poor without interest;
who does not accept a bribe against the innocent.
Whoever does these things
will never be shaken.

Recently, when I went to the hospital to visit someone I did not know well, I encountered an interesting sign on the door: "IMMEDIATE FAMILY ONLY-NO OTHER VISITORS!" It couldn't have been more clear. If you weren't a blood relative, you were not welcome! Even I, as a pastor, could not circumvent this process. Upon peeking my head in the door, I was kindly pointed to the sign and was told I was not welcome. There were rules and regulations, and though I did not fully understand or agree with them, I could not enter!

The opening of this Psalm reminds me of that story, because entering and being in the Presence of the Lord is a restricted activity. Not just anyone can come into His Presence and still live. Sin keeps us from Him, and there is no way to circumvent that process on our own. If you want to be in the Presence of the Lord, you must be blameless. A blameless person is described in pretty clear detail in the rest of the Psalm.

As I read those words, my pride tempts me to say that I am worthy, but my heart tells me the truth. Just as I was sent away from the room, so should I be sent from the Presence of God, for I am far from blameless. I don't always speak truth, sometimes I break my word and I often change my mind. It's the human, sinful part of us on full display when we dare enter the Presence of a Holy God.

But thank God, through Jesus Christ, we have entered into the family of God and have been cleansed of our sin. We no longer depend on our righteousness, but on that of Jesus Christ, and He fits every quality perfectly. By the power of the Spirit, we strive to be what God calls us to be, but it is by the righteousness of Christ that we can enter the Presence of God and not be turned away.

DAY 20
Psalm 73:1-3
**Surely God is good to Israel,
to those who are pure in heart.
But as for me, my feet had almost slipped;
I had nearly lost my foothold.
For I envied the arrogant
when I saw the prosperity of the wicked.**

The words of Psalm 73 could have very easily been written in our own day and age. The truth of God's Word proclaims that those who are called according to His purposes will be rewarded with good coming to them, yet around us it doesn't always seem that way. We see those people who clearly have no need for God prospering. We see those who trust in God faced with trials and tragedies, and everything seems to be out of order. Where is justice? How can this be?

As we wonder about these things, if we are like the Psalmist, we might have our doubts and questions. While we trust God and believe that He is in fact bringing good to those who love Him, our experience may say that it's those who are wicked, those who have no time for God, that are the ones who have life figured out. We may be tempted to base our beliefs not on what we know, but on what is happening around us.

While experience can teach us many things, we can't allow what is happening around us to influence our belief system. Instead, our belief system must influence the way we view the world and what is happening. The truth is that while there may be prosperity for the wicked for a time, eventually all will be set right. God will not allow sin and wickedness to continue, but will restore things as they should be. Yes, for a time, wickedness may prosper, for Satan is currently having his way in this world. But let us not lose our faith, instead, stand firm, trusting that one day all will be set right.

Day 21
Psalm 73:23-26
**Yet I am always with you;
you hold me by my right hand.
You guide me with your counsel,
and afterward you will take me into glory.
Whom have I in heaven but you?
And earth has nothing I desire besides you.
My flesh and my heart may fail,
but God is the strength of my heart
and my portion forever.**

As we read yesterday, Psalm 73 in many ways speaks to the current condition of this world. Around us, all is far from right, and wickedness seems to go unpunished. Those who seek God seem to be foolish, for it is those who seek themselves that seem to have all the fun. But certainly, this will not continue forever. It is far better to trust in God, knowing that in the end all will be set right, and we will be rewarded by remaining in His Presence forever.

The closing words of the Psalm are this reminder. After lamenting the difficult struggle of seeing the wicked prosper, the Psalmist affirms his faith in God. He again places his trust in God, who leads and guides him while he is on this earth and calls him at the end of his life into glory. Perhaps we would do well to remind ourselves of this promise. We often focus on the glory of eternity, but sometimes neglect to understand what the Psalmist clearly states that even on this earth, we have the Lord. We are guided by His counsel and led by His hand.

Nothing, either in eternity or on this earth, can take the place or supersede the Presence of the Lord. No matter what happens, the Lord will strengthen us and be enough for us. The words remind me of the great promise made to us in the book of Romans: For I am convinced that neither death nor life, neither angels nor demons, neither the present nor the future, nor any powers, neither height nor depth, nor anything else in all creation, will be able to separate us from the love of God that is in Christ Jesus our Lord. Today, let us rest in that promise and trust the Lord who will be ours forever.

DAY 22
Psalm 42:1-2
As the deer pants for streams of water,
so my soul pants for you, my God.
My soul thirsts for God, for the living God.
When can I go and meet with God?

The other morning I witnessed an interesting event. My cat, so parched for water, climbed in the bathtub and began lapping up the drips left from previous showers. Obviously, he was thirsty and would do anything to quench his thirst, even if that meant getting into the bathtub and risking a shower! As I watched my cat, that question that I have pondered many times in the past came to mind: "Am I thirsty for the Presence of God?"

That's the question that rises to my mind as I read or sing the words of this Psalm. Do these words characterize my life? In one sense the answer is the same for all of us, we all long for God. Nothing else on this earth can satisfy our deepest thirst for our Creator. Yet, in another sense, sometimes we mask this thirst by seeking to quench it in other ways. Sometimes, we become content with what will not satisfy and what is temporary.

We all need to drink again from Him who offers us living water, the Presence of God. He calls out to us, and beckons all who are thirsty to come to the fountain of His love and mercy. But too often, we are unwilling to allow ourselves to be controlled by the question, "When can I go and meet God?" Instead, we allow the other aspects of our lives to crowd that question out, and take precedence over this most basic activity. We need to seek Him early and often, coming into His Presence not out of duty but out of necessity.

Sometimes this means we will do even what may seem foolish and absurd to others around us. We may delay other things, deny certain invitations, and wake-up early in the morning. If we are truly thirsty for God, as my cat was thirsty for water the other morning, what we do will be guided not by what others think or say, but by our thirst to go and seek after God, who alone can quench our thirst and satisfy our deepest longings!

DAY 23
Psalm 43:5
Why, my soul, are you downcast?
Why so disturbed within me?
Put your hope in God,
for I will yet praise him,
my Savior and my God.

If you are around kids for any amount of time, eventually the infamous question of "why?" will be asked. We usually get frustrated with the fact that this question seems to never cease, and we ultimately say something to the effect of, "Because I said so!" Why is that simple question so troubling and annoying to us? Maybe it is just the repetition of it, but perhaps we avoid that question because it forces us to explore things that we don't completely understand. It might be because the question can't be answered simply and may require some thought.

As we read this verse from Psalm 43, we are confronted with that question yet again, but this time it is being asked of ourselves. The Psalmist wonders at the reason of why he is struggling with thoughts of depression and anxiety. There certainly can be a lot of answers to that question. Many circumstances can cause us to struggle with these feelings, yet that is not the real heart of this question. It goes deeper than that, we must reply to whatever we answer that question with by asking again, "Why?"

When we get deeper into the matter, like the Psalmist, we will conclude that no matter what is causing our fear and anxiety, God is our hope and our strength. He will surely save and deliver us. We read throughout the Psalms that He is our Refuge and our Strength, no harm will come to those who seek shelter in Him.

The problem is, we don't often take the time to explore the "whys" behind how we act and behave. We'd rather wallow in sorrow and sadness, and take anxiety as our constant companion because those things are familiar to us. When those thoughts come, we need to question our own hearts and souls, just as the Psalmist would. We need to peel back the layers with questions of "why," until we can finally realize and resolve that there is no reason to fear, for the solution to our troubles is to put full trust and faith in God.

DAY 24
Psalm 46:1-3
God is our refuge and strength,
an ever-present help in trouble.
Therefore we will not fear, though the earth give way
and the mountains fall into the heart of the sea,
though its waters roar and foam
and the mountains quake with their surging.

Several years ago, I read a book that was particularly transformative in the way I viewed the Presence of God at work in my life. The book, Present Perfect, by Greg Boyd, contains at its core one specific question that we need to be asking ourselves, "Are you awake?" This question is not meant for insomniacs alone, and it's not asking if all this life is a dream. The question instead relates to the presence and works of God in our lives. It reminds us of the truth contained in this Psalm that the Lord is an ever-present God, always with us. It is up to us to be awake and aware of how He is working.

Sometimes I can honestly say, I've drifted off to sleep. I've been so consumed with what I am doing that I've forgotten that the Lord is with me. I've tried to live as my own refuge and strength, or I've sought those things in other ways. I suspect if you're like me, from time to time, you've seemed more like a sleepwalker than someone who is bright-eyed and bushy tailed, aware of how God is moving.

We need to wake-up and become aware that the Lord is with us at each moment, for when we do, the way we operate changes. No longer are we bound by fear of what might happen around us. No longer do we interact with others in ways that dishonor God. If we are aware of the Presence of God with us through the Holy Spirit, it becomes harder and harder to operate outside the will of God. Yes, the call of this Psalm is to be awake and aware that God is not just the God of the past or the future, but the God of the present, who is working in this moment to complete His purposes.

So, are you awake?

DAY 25
Psalm 46:10
He says, "Be still, and know that I am God;
I will be exalted among the nations,
I will be exalted in the earth."

Why does being still scare us so much? Why can't we seem to sit still, alone with our thoughts without the distraction of the phone, the TV, or other people? Is it perhaps that we are afraid of what we might find in the quiet moments? Or perhaps we feel out of control when we can't be busy doing something? Whatever the case, we often avoid stillness and in doing so, we often miss the Presence of God.

In order to find Him, we must be still. We must eliminate distractions and simply wait for Him to come. We must cease all things, so God may enter and show Himself for who He is, the Exalted One, great in all the earth. Stillness alone focuses our minds and hearts and allows us to see God for who He is.

So today, having read those short instructions, let us put them into practice and for this moment, simply be still.

DAY 26
Psalm 50:7-15
"Listen, my people, and I will speak;
I will testify against you, Israel:
I am God, your God.
I bring no charges against you concerning your sacrifices
or concerning your burnt offerings, which are ever before me.
I have no need of a bull from your stall
or of goats from your pens,
for every animal of the forest is mine,
and the cattle on a thousand hills.
I know every bird in the mountains,
and the insects in the fields are mine.
If I were hungry I would not tell you,
for the world is mine, and all that is in it.
Do I eat the flesh of bulls
or drink the blood of goats?
"Sacrifice thank offerings to God,
fulfill your vows to the Most High,
and call on me in the day of trouble;
I will deliver you, and you will honor me."

There is a major difference between religion and relationship. Religion is concerned with rule keeping and doing things out of obligation. In contrast, relationship is about abiding in and being in God's Presence, because it is there that we find love and joy. Religion pressures us to do something more, relationship produces obedience naturally out of our love for God.

The complicated part of the whole discussion is that sometimes the outward actions in either religion or relationship are similar. For example, some people attend worship on a weekly basis out of obligation. They believe that they need to do this to earn God's favor. But others come to worship because they long to be with God's people and enter into the Presence of God. The outward action is the same, but the inward motivation is very different.

It is this inward motivation that we should be constantly examining in our own lives. Why do we do the things we do as we relate to God? Are they done out of obligation or are they done out of thanksgiving? In the Psalm above, the people are faithful in the burnt offerings, but the Lord reminds them that He doesn't need or desire the offerings for the sake of it. He wants them, rather, to come with a sacrifice of thanksgiving as well as with a heart that is full of gratitude.

Though we don't perform burnt offerings today, we can fall into the trap of becoming outwardly religious and neglect our inward relationship with God. When our actions become little more than routine, it is time for us to examine our motivations. We need to rededicate our hearts to the Lord, call on Him with thanksgiving, and ask to reignite our passion for a deep and abiding relationship with Jesus Christ!

DAY 27
Psalm 51:1-6
**Have mercy on me, O God,
according to your unfailing love;
according to your great compassion
blot out my transgressions.
Wash away all my iniquity
and cleanse me from my sin.
For I know my transgressions,
and my sin is always before me.
Against you, you only, have I sinned
and done what is evil in your sight;
so you are right in your verdict
and justified when you judge.
Surely I was sinful at birth,
sinful from the time my mother conceived me.
Yet you desired faithfulness even in the womb;
you taught me wisdom in that secret place.**

Sin, while taking different forms and fashions in our lives, seems to behave in a similar way across the spectrum of humanity. It promises us what we want and until we are confronted with the truth and reality of how terrible it is, we are content to live with it. As the band, Newsboys, said so poetically, the first "taste of sin is always sweet" but then when it is revealed, "it rots in your mouth."

It is the revelation of sin, the rotting taste of a broken relationship with God, which inspired David to pen these beautiful words in the Psalm after his sin with Bathsheba. The words are beautifully broken, truthfully painful, and reveal how terrible sin wrecks and ruins our lives. David, in these words, points out the truth of what we must come to realize, that when we sin our transgression is against God alone. Sin breaks relationship with Him, but God in His great love for us, desires to restore us to right relationship with Him.

This restoration, on the other hand, will not happen unless we fully realize the horror of our sin. Even David, who is called a man after God's own heart, was content with his sin until the prophet Nathan confronted him with the awfulness of it. We, too, need to open our hearts and be ready, so that we might be confronted with sin that clings to our souls. Yes, the process will sometimes be painful. However, it will be far better to remove the rotting death which reigns within us because of sin, and embrace the life that Christ Jesus offers us.

Embracing this life begins by admitting the struggle, and realizing that there is but one way to be cleansed, through the work of God Himself. The only cleansing power is found in the blood of Jesus Christ. So let us open our hearts, confess our sins, and plead for the mercy of God to forgive us and restore our souls.

DAY 28
Psalm 51:10-12
**Create in me a pure heart, O God,
and renew a steadfast spirit within me.
Do not cast me from your presence
or take your Holy Spirit from me.
Restore to me the joy of your salvation
and grant me a willing spirit, to sustain me.**

I grew up singing these words, the praise chorus following very closely to David's prayer for restoration after his sin. The words were set not to a somber tune, but to an upbeat and joyful melody. As I read these words, that music flows through my mind. It reminds me that while there is much pain sometimes, in offering our souls to the Lord and in turning away from our sin, there is much joy in experiencing the restoration of right relationship with God. Being in relationship with Him makes our hearts glad. We want to sing for joy, knowing that His great love for us has cleansed and made us new.

That is the joy of being forgiven, yet it is a joy that should not be taken for granted or abused. The prayer of David here is not demanding or deserving, but of a prayer that leans on the mercy of God. David knows that only God can change a heart. He knows that God alone will decide whether or not to allow David into His Presence. It is up to God, and only He, to sustain David after his sin. So David prays that God will perform these tasks mentioned in Psalm, not because they are deserved, but because the Lord is merciful.

Yes, joy will come to us, but we must remember it is not ours to demand. Instead, it is the Lord's to bestow upon us because of His rich mercy. So like David, as we find joy in knowing that our sins are forgiven, we should also be in awe at this great gift of mercy. We should be in awe that God would choose to sustain us. Our prayer should be that as our hearts are remade, we become His willing servants, those who by the help of the Holy Spirit live in the joy of our salvation, so we might not turn from Him again!

DAY 29
Psalm 52:8-9
**But I am like an olive tree
flourishing in the house of God;
I trust in God's unfailing love
for ever and ever.
For what you have done I will always praise you
in the presence of your faithful people.
And I will hope in your name,
for your name is good.**

Think of all the stuff you own. It will all someday be ruined. There is nothing that cannot be broken, nothing which cannot be destroyed. Even those combs which are called unbreakable are fallible, nothing on this earth is lasting. Think of all the relationships with other people you have. While they may be good at the moment, they will not last forever. Sometimes, disagreements will break them down. Often times people will move, or others, even ourselves, will pass away. It is said that nothing lasts forever, and it is in part true.

I don't write all this to cause our hearts to weep, but to show the great difference that exists between the things of this earth and the steadfastness of our God. In this Psalm, we read about the unfailing love of God. It is a lasting love, a loyal love which endures not just for a season, but forever and ever. Indeed, it is something that will surely last forever! God will never turn away from us, His children. Therefore, we should place our trust in Him. Our hope should be found in nothing less than Jesus Christ!

Yet, though we know things and people are not lasting, it seems that we still turn to them first. We'd rather place our hope in the temporary, as God's love can seem distant. The problem is not the unfailing love of God, the problem is where we are dwelling. If we want to best experience His unfailing love, we need to dwell in His Presence. We need to disregard the other stuff so we might be wholly devoted to the Holy God. Our hope must be in nothing less than Jesus, but it also should not be in anything more either. His unfailing love will surely remain, for all else will pass away!

DAY 30
Psalm 55:22-23
Cast your cares on the Lord
and he will sustain you;
he will never let
the righteous be shaken.
But you, God, will bring down the wicked
into the pit of decay;
the bloodthirsty and deceitful
will not live out half their days.
But as for me, I trust in you.

What are we called to give God? The answer to that question may surprise you. We may think of God as demanding or asking many things from us, His children: sacrifices, praise, worship, honor, and the list could go on and on. We may strive to do all those things, but still neglect the very thing that God desires from us, our cares. He desires that we give Him what we are concerned with, so that He may replace our cares with His sustaining love. God will surely take our cares from us and in exchange, offer us perfect peace. This is the truth that is presented in His Word. But our cares are the one thing that we seem to avoid giving to God.

What is it that hinders us? Sometimes, what concerns us seems, in our eyes, to be of little concern for the God of the universe. Why should we trouble God with such a small matter? If we read of God's care for even the sparrows, we might reconsider what is too minimal for God to handle. Nothing is too small for God to hear, He wants what concerns us, be it small or big. That is the other problem, sometimes our interests may seem too big or too much to ask of God. Surely, the reminder that He has created this universe and holds it in motion, will squash our belief that there is something He cannot handle.

There is this notion that it's too big or too small for God to manage, but neither of these is the case. No matter what we face and are concerned with, we need to give it to God. We need to place our complete trust in Him. We need to do this, not just once and for all, but on a constant basis. It's why Peter's language (1 Peter 5:7 NKJV) reads with "-ing" on the end, because cares come constantly, and we are prone to be anxious and worried about many things. But we need not be, for God will surely accomplish what concerns us. He can take our cares and replace them with perfect peace!

DAY 31
Psalm 120
I call on the Lord in my distress,
and he answers me.
Save me, Lord,
from lying lips
and from deceitful tongues.
What will he do to you,
and what more besides,
you deceitful tongue?
He will punish you with a warrior's sharp arrows,
with burning coals of the broom bush.
Woe to me that I dwell in Meshek,
that I live among the tents of Kedar!
Too long have I lived
among those who hate peace.
I am for peace;
but when I speak, they are for war.

Recently, I had an opportunity to preach on our need for peace. The opening lines of my sermon concentrated on the lack of peace that we seem to experience in our world today. I drew an example from personal experiencing, commenting on the fact that sometimes, my house felt like Meshek or Kedar. All I want is peace, but my kids seem to hate peace! They get into arguments like it is their job sometimes! But as I say those words, I have the proverbial fingers pointing back at me. For I know that I am far from perfect, and sometimes I am the cause of the war in my own household.

It is the truth that rears its ugly head if we are honest with ourselves. As much as we like to play the victim, saying that everyone around us is about war and we are longing for peace, sometimes we are the ones who are causing trouble. Our sinfulness causes dissension just as much as someone else's does, and not one of us is immune to being an instigator of trouble. So perhaps before reading further into this Psalm as the victim, we need to acknowledge our own sinfulness. While we may long for peace, we are selfish, sinful people who need to repent of the war that our own sin wages against peace.

That being said, we can read the words of this Psalm with longing hearts, as well. We can and should be the people who long for peace, calling on Him to intervene in our world. As we experience the struggle in this war-torn world, our hearts must cry out to God, as the Psalmist does, to save us and deliver us from those who lie and create trouble. For God alone will give us peace, and silence our enemies. He alone can defeat the unrest that takes place around us and in our own hearts. So let us today turn away from war and towards God, who is our peace!

DAY 32

Psalm 121
I lift up my eyes to the mountains—
where does my help come from?
My help comes from the Lord,
the Maker of heaven and earth.
He will not let your foot slip—
he who watches over you will not slumber;
indeed, he who watches over Israel
will neither slumber nor sleep.
The Lord watches over you—
the Lord is your shade at your right hand;
the sun will not harm you by day,
nor the moon by night.
The Lord will keep you from all harm—
he will watch over your life;
the Lord will watch over your coming and going
both now and forevermore.

Psalm 121, along with the Psalms around it, were used as a songbook as the people made their way to the temple in Jerusalem. These songs are called the Psalms of Ascent, taken from the way that the people would walk up towards the temple. This traveling songbook gives insight into the thoughts of the people as they made their way to worship the Lord in His holy temple. The opening words of this Psalm paint the picture of what is happening along the journey.

It's said that as people made their way to the temple, they would look around at the hills and mountains and see various shrines to other gods. Here, the Psalmist reminds us that it is not in those things, nor in the mountains or hills that our salvation is found. Instead, we find our hope in the Lord. He is the Creator of all things, and worthy to be praised.

Unlike the idols, who were thought to fall asleep, the Lord is constant in His care for us. He watches over what we do, and is with us no matter where we journey in this life. The people of God reminded themselves of this truth as they went to worship the Lord, that they could go nowhere outside of His watch care.

We, too, in this age where our attention seems to dart here and there, need a reminder of where our trust must be found. It cannot be found in anything other than in Jesus Christ. He alone is the Lord who can protect us, keep us from harm, and watch over us in all times and in all seasons of life. Perhaps today, we should pray a simple prayer, that He would keep us in His watchcare no matter what journey this day leads us on.

DAY 33
Psalm 139:7-12
Where can I go from Your Spirit?
Or where can I flee from Your presence?
If I ascend into heaven, You are there;
If I make my bed in hell, behold, You are there.
If I take the wings of the morning,
And dwell in the uttermost parts of the sea,
Even there Your hand shall lead me,
And Your right hand shall hold me.
If I say, "Surely the darkness shall fall on me,"
Even the night shall be light about me;
Indeed, the darkness shall not hide from You,
But the night shines as the day;
The darkness and the light are both alike to You.

Maybe you've heard the phrase before, "You can run, but you can't hide." It is meant to strike fear in our hearts, and it is often used by an evil villain as a way to intimidate his or her target. Though the phrase is often disconcerting, sometimes it can be comforting to us. In these verses, it is presented in terms of our God, who is always with us, no matter where we go. We cannot escape His Presence, we can neither run nor hide from Him.

Sometimes in life, we try to run away. We want to be far from God, for we feel as if we know better than Him. When something goes wrong, when we face grief, sorrow, or loss, we believe the best place to be is without Him. But it is foolish to believe that we can avoid Him, outrun Him, or hide from Him. He is always with us, there is no place He cannot be. Even if we do not sense Him, that does not mean that He is not there. Rather than try and avoid Him, we should embrace Him, and give our hearts to Him. For His purpose in being with us is not to bring us harm, but to lead and guide us, like a shepherd who cares for his sheep.

The idea that God is always there is overwhelming, as we think of all the places we travel to both physically and mentally. We go from moments of joy to moments of sorrow. Our lives can move from heavenly bliss to what seems to be hell on earth in a matter of hours. We can be anxious and overwhelmed, especially at the darkest moments in life. However, we can be comforted by the fact that we are not alone. Our God will never leave us or forsake us. His hand will lead and hold us, and He will protect and keep us in His perfect love, which comes through Jesus Christ.

DAY 34
Psalm 31:1-5
In you, Lord, I have taken refuge;
let me never be put to shame;
deliver me in your righteousness.
Turn your ear to me,
come quickly to my rescue;
be my rock of refuge,
a strong fortress to save me.
Since you are my rock and my fortress,
for the sake of your name lead and guide me.
Keep me free from the trap that is set for me,
for you are my refuge.
Into your hands I commit my spirit;
deliver me, Lord, my faithful God.

When I first became a pastor, I began preaching from the first book of the Bible, Genesis. In that book, several significant life themes are revealed to us, one of them being that God is in control. It is with these words that I encouraged my congregation. Just as well, I still frequently remind myself of these words when my life seems to spin out of control. I need not fear, for the Lord can handle all things and nothing escapes His guidance or control.

Although I remind myself of that truth, I also consider how difficult it is to live it out. Perhaps it is because we often refuse to let go of what is not really ours to begin with. We struggle with laying everything down before the Lord. Sin has lodged so deep in our minds, that we feel the best way to live is to hold tightly onto some part of our lives. Yet, we must remember to surrender ourselves to the Lord.

Yes, we must place our lives again in the hands of our Creator if we are to experience the deliverance and the peace that He alone can offer us. It makes no sense to enter the refuge of the Lord if we will refuse to enter fully. We cannot hold back, for it is all or nothing. We must fully devote ourselves to the Lord, commend our lives into His hands, and submit our control to the One who ultimately has it anyway.

We can take comfort as we surrender all to the Lord. He is not only in control, He is faithful to His promises, and His love for us will endure forever. As He exercises dominion over the universe, He is using all things to bring us good and conform us in the image of His son, Jesus Christ. So today, as with every day, it's time to let go. For God, not us, is in control!

DAY 35
Psalm 31:6-8
**I hate those who cling to worthless idols;
as for me, I trust in the Lord.
I will be glad and rejoice in your love,
for you saw my affliction
and knew the anguish of my soul.
You have not given me into the hands of the enemy
but have set my feet in a spacious place.**

It seems pretty foolish to place your trust in something that you made with your own hands. Think about it, something that is crafted by your own hands, somehow becomes alive and deserves your worship? It really doesn't make sense. Yet, somehow, we still seem to cling to worthless idols. They don't take the form of metal or wood, but instead involve the ideas of power, money, or even ourselves. When we set these things up in the place of the Lord, we are no better than those people who bow before inanimate objects and place trust in what does not save.

Rather than cling to materialistic objects, we should cling instead to the Lord. For the Lord is not like the worthless idols who cannot see, hear, or care for us. No, the Lord instead sees what we are facing, and knows us intimately. He not only sees and knows us, out of His great love for us, He chooses to protect us and rescue us. Unlike the worthless idols, which can do nothing for us, the Living God looks upon us with love. He has the power to save, and exercises that power for His children.

Like the Psalmist, we must reject the sin of idolatry and guard our hearts against that which is worthless. We must ask ourselves what we are trusting in, and if the answer is not the Lord, and Him alone, we must refocus our hearts! As the Lord delivers us, we must not be silent. We should be glad and rejoice, for our act of worship will not only please the Lord, but it will be a witness to the world around us that the Lord alone has the power to save us!

ROBERT W. RICE

DAY 36
Psalm 31:9-13
Be merciful to me, Lord, for I am in distress;
my eyes grow weak with sorrow,
my soul and body with grief.
My life is consumed by anguish
and my years by groaning;
my strength fails because of my affliction,
and my bones grow weak.
Because of all my enemies,
I am the utter contempt of my neighbors
and an object of dread to my closest friends—
those who see me on the street flee from me.
I am forgotten as though I were dead;
I have become like broken pottery.
For I hear many whispering,
"Terror on every side!"
They conspire against me
and plot to take my life.

The hymn, "Let Us Break Bread Together," is reserved exclusively it seems for communion Sundays. Even then, sometimes it finds its place only in an instrumental form as the bread and cup are passed. But its words, in particular the last line, should find lodging in our hearts and be a constant prayer on our lips, "O Lord, have mercy on me!" This is the prayer that opens this section of the thirty-first Psalm, a cry for deliverance and for God to show mercy to the Psalmist.

As sinners, we desperately need the mercy of God. We need this gift of God to show us His loving-kindness not just day by day, but hour by hour. We need to fall on our knees and cry out for the mercy of God because of the broken and sin-sick nature of this world in which we live. Our world is shattered and the remedy cannot come from within us, only from the Lord, Himself. So as the Psalmist writes, be merciful, Lord.

We need the Lord to come close to us in the moments of trouble like we read about in this Psalm. Only His love and His mercy can sustain us. We can take heart knowing that God will surely be with us and will understand the pain we are facing. For if you read the words of this Psalm, and think of what Jesus faced here on earth, you will, like me, remember what happened as Jesus neared the end of His life. Constantly in the Gospels, we read that people plotted to kill Jesus. He knew what it was like to face opposition, persecution, even torture, and He did it so God might reveal His mercy to us.

So in our pain, Jesus can and does understand what we are facing. He not only understands, He experienced this pain, so He might be able to provide mercy to us. For He, by the power of the cross, displayed God's greatest act of mercy: His deep love for us. So without a doubt, we can call out for His mercy, and look to Him as the one who can provide mercy and forgiveness for our sins.

DAY 37
Psalm 31:14-18
**But I trust in you, Lord;
I say, "You are my God."
My times are in your hands;
deliver me from the hands of my enemies,
from those who pursue me.
Let your face shine on your servant;
save me in your unfailing love.
Let me not be put to shame, Lord,
for I have cried out to you;
but let the wicked be put to shame
and be silent in the realm of the dead.
Let their lying lips be silenced,
for with pride and contempt
they speak arrogantly against the righteous.**

Time is a funny thing. Sometimes it races, sometimes it drags. It is often those moments that we enjoy that seem to fly away too quickly, while painful moments seem to last an eternity. I've often wondered how Jesus, the one who holds time in His hands, experienced time as He prepared for His final moments before the cross. Did time go quickly or did it stand still? Did it feel like a weight upon Him or did He long for a few more minutes with the disciples?

Whatever the case, He knew that the timing of it all was perfect. His times and His mission were secure in the hands of God the Father. Jesus recognized that, and though He struggled in agony at the weight of what was to come in the Garden, He entrusted Himself to the will and plan of God.

We would do well to recognize that same truth, the one that is proclaimed in this Psalm, that each moment and every second of every day are in the hands of the Lord. His plan is perfect, and we should submit to it. That is not to say there will not be moments of struggle. Surely we can ask for deliverance and we can pray for freedom from pain, but ultimately, like Jesus did in the Garden, one statement must ring from our heart: "Thy will be done!"

His will must be done, because as the Psalmist so rightfully declares, "He is God, and we are not!"

DAY 38: Maundy Thursday
Psalm 41:9
Even my close friend,
someone I trusted,
one who shared my bread,
has turned against me.

He knew. It was no secret to Jesus that Judas would betray Him and sell Him out to the Jewish authorities for thirty pieces of silver. Yet, Jesus still called Judas to be one of His disciples. He still allowed Judas to be part of His closest followers and friends, and because of this, the pain of Judas' choice cut especially deep. It is one thing to be betrayed, it is another to have someone you love be the one who turns against you.

We may or may not know some of the pain that Jesus felt when He was betrayed. Some of us, surely, have had people turn on us. Some of us have felt abandoned by those we thought loved us. But none of us is in the position that Jesus was in, for none of us is completely innocent as He was. Even if we can find comparative experiences in our lives, we can't fully comprehend just how difficult that night was for Jesus, when He was betrayed by Judas.

And perhaps because we cannot fathom it, we often look at Judas with a glare in our eyes and the thought, "How could you?" It's a raw and honest question, and perhaps we will never fully understand the deep motives of Judas's sin-sick heart that was fed by the monster of greed. However, we shouldn't direct the question at this man who history calls the worst sinner, rather we should direct it at ourselves.

For if we are honest, if we look in the proverbial mirror, we will find ourselves as the ones who have betrayed our Savior. We have turned to ourselves rather than to honor Him, we have claimed that we do not know Him, and we have sold Him out for material things. Today, as we race towards the moment of Jesus' death, let us not look at the betrayal that runs in the hearts of others, but let us confess and repent of our own!

ROBERT W. RICE

DAY 39: Good Friday
Psalm 22:1, 12-18

My God, my God, why have you forsaken me?
Why are you so far from saving me,
so far from my cries of anguish?
Many bulls surround me;
strong bulls of Bashan encircle me.
Roaring lions that tear their prey
open their mouths wide against me.
I am poured out like water,
and all my bones are out of joint.
My heart has turned to wax;
it has melted within me.
My mouth is dried up like a potsherd,
and my tongue sticks to the roof of my mouth;
you lay me in the dust of death.
Dogs surround me,
a pack of villains encircles me;
they pierce my hands and my feet.
All my bones are on display;
people stare and gloat over me.
They divide my clothes among them
and cast lots for my garment.

Psalm 22 opens with the very words that Jesus cried from the cross in agony as He was crucified: "My God, my God, why have You forsaken me..." This Psalm offers a perfect description of the horror that was His crucifixion. We cannot overestimate that pain and difficulty that Jesus endured in His physical body on the cross so long ago.

His dignity was nonexistent, as He hung completely naked before the crowd. His body, covered in both fresh and dried blood, ached in every way. His mouth was completely dried and required water, which never came to Him. His bones were disjointed and protruded from the skin that hung loose and out of place. Searing pain became His constant companion, with each labored breath, it pulsed throughout His body.

The Psalm poetically tells the story of the cross, reminding us of the pain endured by our Savior, Jesus Christ, at Calvary. Yet the physical pain, great as it was, paled in comparison to the spiritual abandonment that Jesus felt that day. There He was, the very Son of God who had dwelt with the Father in perfect relationship since eternity past, feeling as if God had turned His face away. This was the weight of sin upon His shoulders.

On that cross as Jesus died, He, who knew no sin, became sin so that we may live again. With that decision, the penalty for all our sins was paid. It was finished, the work which brought us redemption and sealed by the shedding of His blood. We know that to be true, yet perhaps we do not allow ourselves to realize the value of it. We are unwilling for at least a moment to dwell in the pain of Christ, to recognize the value of it, and to see His depth of love for us.

Let us on this day that brings us everything, open our hearts. Let us feel the pain of sin and weep as we see the man upon our cross, our sin upon His shoulders. Then rise and know that our redemption is complete, for the price has been paid, and the victory is soon to be won.

DAY 40: Holy Saturday
Psalm 22:19
But you, Lord, do not be far from me.
You are my strength; come quickly to help me.

We might think of Good Friday, the day of the crucifixion, as the darkest day in history. It appeared by all accounts, that hope was lost. The women wept at the cross, the disciples huddled in hiding, unsure of what the future would bring. All seemed lost. The feeling is described in the song, "Forever," by Kari Jobe:

The moon and stars they wept
The morning sun was dead
The Savior of the world was fallen
His body on the cross
His blood poured out for us
The weight of every curse upon Him
One final breath He gave
As heaven looked away

Yet, perhaps Saturday seemed like an even darker day. Was it Saturday that the reality began to set in? Was it the moment when the darkness closed in on the people, as Jesus' body lay in that stone cold tomb? I can only imagine how difficult it was to think that all hope was lost.

The Son of God was laid in darkness.

In moments of darkness in our own lives, perhaps we experience a little bit of this emotion. We may feel as if hope is lost after the darkness begins to set in, like our hearts will be filled with this depth of pain forever. It is in these moments, that we must hold fast to our faith, and we must remember that even these moments of pain can produce good in our lives. Consider how much brighter the day is after we endure a time of darkness. Imagine the power of Jesus at work in what appeared still as darkness:

A battle in the grave
The war on death was waged
The power of hell forever broken.

In the darkness, may hope be our constant companion. May God strengthen us as we wait for Him to quickly come. May we know that weeping lingers for a time, but joy will come in the morning.

Easter Sunday
Psalm 150
Praise the Lord.
Praise God in his sanctuary;
praise him in his mighty heavens.
Praise him for his acts of power;
praise him for his surpassing greatness.
Praise him with the sounding of the trumpet,
praise him with the harp and lyre,
praise him with timbrel and dancing,
praise him with the strings and pipe,
praise him with the clash of cymbals,
praise him with resounding cymbals.
Let everything that has breath praise the Lord.
Praise the Lord.

Yes, today let us praise the Lord. Let us give Him thanks and glory, for we know that our Savior lives. On that Resurrection Morn, the words that we began to read yesterday from the song, "Forever," come to a beautiful culmination of praise:

The ground began to shake
The stone was rolled away
His perfect love could not be overcome
Now death where is your sting?
Our resurrected King
Has rendered You defeated

Forever, He is glorified
Forever, He is lifted high
Forever, He is risen
He is alive and therefore
We sing Hallelujah

ABOUT THE AUTHOR

Reverend Robert W. Rice and his wife Jen live in Muncy, Pennsylvania with their four children Alexa, Kaylyn, Cole and Cohen, where Rob serves as the pastor of Muncy Baptist Church. His desire in all things is to draw people closer to God, and this project, is a continuation of that desire, born out of a daily devotional blog that Rob writes weekdays for his congregation. To contact Rob or find out more about his writings go to drawingclosertogod. wordpress.com or email him at pastor.rwrice@gmail.com

Made in the USA
Middletown, DE
01 February 2017